THIS

FOOD DIARY

BELONGS TO:

_____

DATE:

_____

A food diary may help you and your doctor keep track of any triggers and manage your condition. Always discuss your conditions with a doctor or health professional. Good Luck!

YOUR
FOOD DIARY

Use this book to help identify and eliminate triggers that could be causing or exacerbating your problem.

→ Complete the following DAY 1 to DAY 7 pages to track food, drink and symptoms for each day

→ At the end of each DAY 7, complete a WEEKLY TRIGGER and SUMMARY page to provide an overview of that particular week

→ Choose to record data for one week or up to four weeks - it's up to you

→ After you have completed the amount of weeks you have chosen to keep your diary, use the TRIGGERS ROUND-UP pages to record all the biggest triggers you have found

→ Use the blank lined pages at the back of the book for additional notes and thoughts

WEEK ONE

DAY 1 - WEEK 1 Breakfast/Lunch

Date ___ / ___ / ___

Food/Drink	Time ___:___	Reaction
BREAKFAST		Y / N
		Y / N
		Y / N
		Y / N

Symptoms:

Comfort Level 1= normal 10= very uncomfortable ① ② ③ ④ ⑤ ⑥ ⑦ ⑧ ⑨ ⑩

Notes:

Medication: _____ Supplements: _____

Food/Drink	Time ___:___	Reaction
LUNCH		Y / N
		Y / N
		Y / N
		Y / N

Symptoms:

Comfort Level 1= normal 10= very uncomfortable ① ② ③ ④ ⑤ ⑥ ⑦ ⑧ ⑨ ⑩

Notes:

Medication: _____ Supplements: _____

DAY 1 - WEEK 1 — Dinner/Snacks/Sleep/Wellbeing

Food/Drink   Time ____ : ____   **Reaction**

DINNER

	Reaction
	Y / N
	Y / N
	Y / N
	Y / N

Symptoms:

Comfort Level 1= normal 10= very uncomfortable ① ② ③ ④ ⑤ ⑥ ⑦ ⑧ ⑨ ⑩

Notes:

Medication: Supplements:

Food/Drink   **Reaction**

SNACKS

	Reaction
	Y / N
	Y / N
	Y / N

Symptoms:

Comfort Level 1= normal 10= very uncomfortable ① ② ③ ④ ⑤ ⑥ ⑦ ⑧ ⑨ ⑩

Daily Bowel Movements:
ie: watery, soft, normal, hard etc.

Sleep from: :   **to:**   :   ☐ /hours

Exercise: Cardio Y / N   Weights Y / N

Daily stress Level: (1= calm 10= very stressed)
① ② ③ ④ ⑤ ⑥ ⑦ ⑧ ⑨ ⑩

DAY 2 - WEEK 1 Breakfast/Lunch

Date ___ / ___ / ___

Food/Drink	Time ___:___	Reaction
BREAKFAST		Y / N
		Y / N
		Y / N
		Y / N

Symptoms:

Comfort Level 1= normal 10= very uncomfortable ① ② ③ ④ ⑤ ⑥ ⑦ ⑧ ⑨ ⑩

Notes:

Medication: Supplements:

Food/Drink	Time ___:___	Reaction
LUNCH		Y / N
		Y / N
		Y / N
		Y / N

Symptoms:

Comfort Level 1= normal 10= very uncomfortable ① ② ③ ④ ⑤ ⑥ ⑦ ⑧ ⑨ ⑩

Notes:

Medication: Supplements:

Food/Drink	Time ____ : ____	Reaction	Symptoms:
DINNER		Y / N	
		Y / N	
		Y / N	
		Y / N	

Comfort Level 1= normal 10= very uncomfortable → ① ② ③ ④ ⑤ ⑥ ⑦ ⑧ ⑨ ⑩

Notes:

Medication: Supplements:

Food/Drink	Reaction	Symptoms:
SNACKS	Y / N	
	Y / N	
	Y / N	

Comfort Level 1= normal 10= very uncomfortable → ① ② ③ ④ ⑤ ⑥ ⑦ ⑧ ⑨ ⑩

Daily Bowel Movements:
ie: watery, soft, normal, hard etc.

Sleep from: :   to: :   ☐ /hours

Exercise: Cardio Y / N   Weights Y / N

Daily stress Level: (1= calm 10= very stressed)
① ② ③ ④ ⑤ ⑥ ⑦ ⑧ ⑨ ⑩

Food/Drink	Time ____ : ____	Reaction
BREAKFAST		Y / N
		Y / N
		Y / N
		Y / N

Symptoms:

Comfort Level 1= normal 10= very uncomfortable ➜ (1)(2)(3)(4)(5)(6)(7)(8)(9)(10)

Notes:

Medication: Supplements:

Food/Drink	Time ____ : ____	Reaction
LUNCH		Y / N
		Y / N
		Y / N
		Y / N

Symptoms:

Comfort Level 1= normal 10= very uncomfortable ➜ (1)(2)(3)(4)(5)(6)(7)(8)(9)(10)

Notes:

Medication: Supplements:

Food/Drink	Time ____ : ____	Reaction
DINNER		Y / N
		Y / N
		Y / N
		Y / N

Symptoms:

Comfort Level 1= normal 10= very uncomfortable ① ② ③ ④ ⑤ ⑥ ⑦ ⑧ ⑨ ⑩

Notes:

Medication: _____   Supplements: _____

Food/Drink	Reaction
SNACKS	Y / N
	Y / N
	Y / N

Symptoms:

Comfort Level 1= normal 10= very uncomfortable ① ② ③ ④ ⑤ ⑥ ⑦ ⑧ ⑨ ⑩

Daily Bowel Movements:
ie: watery, soft, normal, hard etc.

Sleep from: ___ : ___ to: ___ : ___ ☐ /hours

Exercise: Cardio Y / N   Weights Y / N

Daily stress Level: (1= calm 10= very stressed)
① ② ③ ④ ⑤ ⑥ ⑦ ⑧ ⑨ ⑩

DAY 4 - WEEK 1 Breakfast/Lunch

Date ____ / ____ / ____

Food/Drink	Time ____ : ____	Reaction
BREAKFAST		Y / N
		Y / N
		Y / N
		Y / N

Symptoms:

Comfort Level 1= normal 10= very uncomfortable   ① ② ③ ④ ⑤ ⑥ ⑦ ⑧ ⑨ ⑩

Notes:

Medication: _____ Supplements: _____

Food/Drink	Time ____ : ____	Reaction
LUNCH		Y / N
		Y / N
		Y / N
		Y / N

Symptoms:

Comfort Level 1= normal 10= very uncomfortable ① ② ③ ④ ⑤ ⑥ ⑦ ⑧ ⑨ ⑩

Notes:

Medication: _____ Supplements: _____

Food/Drink Time ___ : ___	Reaction	Symptoms:
DINNER	Y / N	
	Y / N	
	Y / N	
	Y / N	

Comfort Level 1= normal 10= very uncomfortable → ① ② ③ ④ ⑤ ⑥ ⑦ ⑧ ⑨ ⑩

Notes:

Medication: Supplements:

Food/Drink	Reaction	Symptoms:
SNACKS	Y / N	
	Y / N	
	Y / N	

Comfort Level 1= normal 10= very uncomfortable → ① ② ③ ④ ⑤ ⑥ ⑦ ⑧ ⑨ ⑩

Daily Bowel Movements:
ie: watery, soft, normal, hard etc.

Sleep from: :   to: :   ☐ /hours

Exercise: Cardio Y / N   Weights Y / N

Daily stress Level: (1= calm 10= very stressed)

① ② ③ ④ ⑤ ⑥ ⑦ ⑧ ⑨ ⑩

DAY 5 - WEEK 1 Breakfast/Lunch   Date   /   /

Food/Drink	Time ___:___	Reaction
BREAKFAST		Y / N
		Y / N
		Y / N
		Y / N

Symptoms:

Comfort Level 1= normal 10= very uncomfortable ① ② ③ ④ ⑤ ⑥ ⑦ ⑧ ⑨ ⑩

Notes:

Medication: Supplements:

Food/Drink	Time ___:___	Reaction
LUNCH		Y / N
		Y / N
		Y / N
		Y / N

Symptoms:

Comfort Level 1= normal 10= very uncomfortable ① ② ③ ④ ⑤ ⑥ ⑦ ⑧ ⑨ ⑩

Notes:

Medication: Supplements:

Food/Drink	Time ___ : ___	Reaction	Symptoms:
DINNER		Y / N	
		Y / N	
		Y / N	
		Y / N	

Comfort Level 1= normal 10= very uncomfortable → ① ② ③ ④ ⑤ ⑥ ⑦ ⑧ ⑨ ⑩

Notes:

Medication: Supplements:

Food/Drink	Reaction	Symptoms:
SNACKS	Y / N	
	Y / N	
	Y / N	

Comfort Level 1= normal 10= very uncomfortable → ① ② ③ ④ ⑤ ⑥ ⑦ ⑧ ⑨ ⑩

Daily Bowel Movements:
ie: watery, soft, normal, hard etc.

Sleep from: :   to: :   ☐ /hours

Exercise: Cardio Y / N   Weights Y / N

Daily stress Level: (1= calm 10= very stressed)
① ② ③ ④ ⑤ ⑥ ⑦ ⑧ ⑨ ⑩

DAY 6 - WEEK 1 Breakfast/Lunch

Date ___ / ___ / ___

Food/Drink	Time ___ : ___	Reaction
BREAKFAST		Y / N
		Y / N
		Y / N
		Y / N

Symptoms:

Comfort Level 1= normal 10= very uncomfortable ① ② ③ ④ ⑤ ⑥ ⑦ ⑧ ⑨ ⑩

Notes:

Medication: _____ Supplements: _____

Food/Drink	Time ___ : ___	Reaction
LUNCH		Y / N
		Y / N
		Y / N
		Y / N

Symptoms:

Comfort Level 1= normal 10= very uncomfortable ① ② ③ ④ ⑤ ⑥ ⑦ ⑧ ⑨ ⑩

Notes:

Medication: _____ Supplements: _____

Food/Drink	Time ___ : ___	Reaction	Symptoms:
DINNER		Y / N	
		Y / N	
		Y / N	
		Y / N	

Comfort Level 1= normal 10= very uncomfortable ⟶ ① ② ③ ④ ⑤ ⑥ ⑦ ⑧ ⑨ ⑩

Notes:

Medication: Supplements:

Food/Drink	Reaction	Symptoms:
SNACKS	Y / N	
	Y / N	
	Y / N	

Comfort Level 1= normal 10= very uncomfortable ⟶ ① ② ③ ④ ⑤ ⑥ ⑦ ⑧ ⑨ ⑩

Daily Bowel Movements:
ie: watery, soft, normal, hard etc.

Sleep from: :   **to:**   :   ☐ /hours

Exercise: Cardio Y / N   Weights Y / N

Daily stress Level: (1= calm 10= very stressed)
① ② ③ ④ ⑤ ⑥ ⑦ ⑧ ⑨ ⑩

DAY 7 - WEEK 1 Breakfast/Lunch

Date   /   /

Food/Drink	Time ____ : ____	Reaction
BREAKFAST		Y / N
		Y / N
		Y / N
		Y / N

Symptoms:

Comfort Level   1= normal   10= very uncomfortable   ① ② ③ ④ ⑤ ⑥ ⑦ ⑧ ⑨ ⑩

Notes:

Medication: Supplements:

Food/Drink	Time ____ : ____	Reaction
LUNCH		Y / N
		Y / N
		Y / N
		Y / N

Symptoms:

Comfort Level   1= normal   10= very uncomfortable   ① ② ③ ④ ⑤ ⑥ ⑦ ⑧ ⑨ ⑩

Notes:

Medication: Supplements:

Food/Drink	Time ___ : ___	Reaction	Symptoms:
DINNER		Y / N	
		Y / N	
		Y / N	
		Y / N	

Comfort Level 1= normal 10= very uncomfortable → ① ② ③ ④ ⑤ ⑥ ⑦ ⑧ ⑨ ⑩

Notes:

Medication: Supplements:

Food/Drink	Reaction	Symptoms:
SNACKS	Y / N	
	Y / N	
	Y / N	

Comfort Level 1= normal 10= very uncomfortable → ① ② ③ ④ ⑤ ⑥ ⑦ ⑧ ⑨ ⑩

Daily Bowel Movements:
ie: watery, soft, normal, hard etc.

Sleep from: :   to: :   ☐ /hours

Exercise: Cardio Y / N   Weights Y / N

Daily stress Level: (1= calm 10= very stressed)
① ② ③ ④ ⑤ ⑥ ⑦ ⑧ ⑨ ⑩

Flick through last week's reports and list out any food, drink or activities that are affecting your condition. The items you list here will provide a summary of triggers you experienced during the week.

Food/Drink

_____

_____

_____

_____

_____

_____

_____

_____

Activity

_____

_____

_____

_____

_____

_____

_____

Tomorrow is a new day!

WEEK 1   SUMMARY

How has your week been?
Will you be making any changes for next week?

How have you been feeling overall this past week?

WEEK TWO

DAY 1 - WEEK 2 Breakfast/Lunch

Date / /

Food/Drink	Time ___ : ___	Reaction	Symptoms:
BREAKFAST		Y / N	
		Y / N	
		Y / N	
		Y / N	

Comfort Level 1= normal 10= very uncomfortable ① ② ③ ④ ⑤ ⑥ ⑦ ⑧ ⑨ ⑩

Notes:

Medication: Supplements:

Food/Drink	Time ___ : ___	Reaction	Symptoms:
LUNCH		Y / N	
		Y / N	
		Y / N	
		Y / N	

Comfort Level 1= normal 10= very uncomfortable ① ② ③ ④ ⑤ ⑥ ⑦ ⑧ ⑨ ⑩

Notes:

Medication: Supplements:

Food/Drink	Time ___:___	Reaction	Symptoms:
DINNER		Y / N	
		Y / N	
		Y / N	
		Y / N	

Comfort Level 1= normal 10= very uncomfortable ① ② ③ ④ ⑤ ⑥ ⑦ ⑧ ⑨ ⑩

Notes:

Medication: Supplements:

Food/Drink		Reaction	Symptoms:
SNACKS		Y / N	
		Y / N	
		Y / N	

Comfort Level 1= normal 10= very uncomfortable ① ② ③ ④ ⑤ ⑥ ⑦ ⑧ ⑨ ⑩

Daily Bowel Movements:
ie: watery, soft, normal, hard etc.

Sleep from: :   to: :   ☐ /hours

Exercise: Cardio Y / N   Weights Y / N

Daily stress Level: (1= calm 10= very stressed)
① ② ③ ④ ⑤ ⑥ ⑦ ⑧ ⑨ ⑩

DAY 2 - WEEK 2 Breakfast/Lunch

Date ___ / ___ / ___

Food/Drink	Time ___:___	Reaction
BREAKFAST		Y / N
		Y / N
		Y / N
		Y / N

Symptoms:

Comfort Level 1= normal 10= very uncomfortable → ① ② ③ ④ ⑤ ⑥ ⑦ ⑧ ⑨ ⑩

Notes:

Medication: Supplements:

Food/Drink	Time ___:___	Reaction
LUNCH		Y / N
		Y / N
		Y / N
		Y / N

Symptoms:

Comfort Level 1= normal 10= very uncomfortable → ① ② ③ ④ ⑤ ⑥ ⑦ ⑧ ⑨ ⑩

Notes:

Medication: Supplements:

DAY 2 - WEEK 2   Dinner/Snacks/Sleep/Wellbeing

Food/Drink	Time ___:___	Reaction	Symptoms:
DINNER		Y / N	
		Y / N	
		Y / N	
		Y / N	

Comfort Level 1= normal 10= very uncomfortable ① ② ③ ④ ⑤ ⑥ ⑦ ⑧ ⑨ ⑩

Notes:

Medication: Supplements:

Food/Drink	Reaction	Symptoms:
SNACKS	Y / N	
	Y / N	
	Y / N	

Comfort Level 1= normal 10= very uncomfortable ① ② ③ ④ ⑤ ⑥ ⑦ ⑧ ⑨ ⑩

Daily Bowel Movements:
ie: watery, soft, normal, hard etc.

Sleep from: :   to: :   ☐ /hours

Exercise: Cardio Y / N   Weights Y / N

Daily stress Level: (1= calm 10= very stressed)
① ② ③ ④ ⑤ ⑥ ⑦ ⑧ ⑨ ⑩

DAY 3 - WEEK 2 Breakfast/Lunch

Date ___ / ___ / ___

Food/Drink	Time ___:___	Reaction
BREAKFAST		Y / N
		Y / N
		Y / N
		Y / N

Symptoms:

Comfort Level 1= normal 10= very uncomfortable → ① ② ③ ④ ⑤ ⑥ ⑦ ⑧ ⑨ ⑩

Notes:

Medication: _____ Supplements: _____

Food/Drink	Time ___:___	Reaction
LUNCH		Y / N
		Y / N
		Y / N
		Y / N

Symptoms:

Comfort Level 1= normal 10= very uncomfortable → ① ② ③ ④ ⑤ ⑥ ⑦ ⑧ ⑨ ⑩

Notes:

Medication: _____ Supplements: _____

Food/Drink	Time ____ : ____	Reaction	Symptoms:
DINNER		Y / N	
		Y / N	
		Y / N	
		Y / N	

Comfort Level 1= normal 10= very uncomfortable ➔ ① ② ③ ④ ⑤ ⑥ ⑦ ⑧ ⑨ ⑩

Notes:

Medication: **Supplements:**

Food/Drink	Reaction	Symptoms:
SNACKS	Y / N	
	Y / N	
	Y / N	

Comfort Level 1= normal 10= very uncomfortable ➔ ① ② ③ ④ ⑤ ⑥ ⑦ ⑧ ⑨ ⑩

Daily Bowel Movements:
ie: watery, soft, normal, hard etc.

Sleep from: ___ : ___ **to:** ___ : ___ ☐ /hours

Exercise: Cardio Y / N   Weights Y / N

Daily stress Level: (1= calm 10= very stressed)
① ② ③ ④ ⑤ ⑥ ⑦ ⑧ ⑨ ⑩

DAY 4 - WEEK 2 Breakfast/Lunch

Date ___/___/___

Food/Drink	Time ___:___	Reaction
BREAKFAST		Y / N
		Y / N
		Y / N
		Y / N

Symptoms:

Comfort Level 1= normal 10= very uncomfortable ➜ ① ② ③ ④ ⑤ ⑥ ⑦ ⑧ ⑨ ⑩

Notes:

Medication: _____ Supplements: _____

Food/Drink	Time ___:___	Reaction
LUNCH		Y / N
		Y / N
		Y / N
		Y / N

Symptoms:

Comfort Level 1= normal 10= very uncomfortable ➜ ① ② ③ ④ ⑤ ⑥ ⑦ ⑧ ⑨ ⑩

Notes:

Medication: _____ Supplements: _____

Food/Drink   Time ____ : ____ | **Reaction** | **Symptoms:**

DINNER

	Reaction
	Y / N
	Y / N
	Y / N
	Y / N

Comfort Level 1= normal 10= very uncomfortable   ① ② ③ ④ ⑤ ⑥ ⑦ ⑧ ⑨ ⑩

Notes:

Medication: Supplements:

Food/Drink | **Reaction** | **Symptoms:**

SNACKS

	Reaction
	Y / N
	Y / N
	Y / N

Comfort Level 1= normal 10= very uncomfortable   ① ② ③ ④ ⑤ ⑥ ⑦ ⑧ ⑨ ⑩

Daily Bowel Movements:
ie: watery, soft, normal, hard etc.

Sleep from: :   **to:**   :   ☐ /hours

Exercise: Cardio Y / N   Weights Y / N

Daily stress Level: (1= calm 10= very stressed)
① ② ③ ④ ⑤ ⑥ ⑦ ⑧ ⑨ ⑩

DAY 5 - WEEK 2 Breakfast/Lunch   Date   /   /

Food/Drink	Time ___ : ___	Reaction	Symptoms:
BREAKFAST		Y / N	
		Y / N	
		Y / N	
		Y / N	

Comfort Level 1= normal 10= very uncomfortable ① ② ③ ④ ⑤ ⑥ ⑦ ⑧ ⑨ ⑩

Notes:

Medication: Supplements:

Food/Drink	Time ___ : ___	Reaction	Symptoms:
LUNCH		Y / N	
		Y / N	
		Y / N	
		Y / N	

Comfort Level 1= normal 10= very uncomfortable ① ② ③ ④ ⑤ ⑥ ⑦ ⑧ ⑨ ⑩

Notes:

Medication: Supplements:

DAY 5 - WEEK 2 — Dinner/Snacks/Sleep/Wellbeing

Food/Drink	Time ___ : ___	Reaction	Symptoms:
DINNER		Y / N	
		Y / N	
		Y / N	
		Y / N	

Comfort Level 1= normal 10= very uncomfortable ① ② ③ ④ ⑤ ⑥ ⑦ ⑧ ⑨ ⑩

Notes:

Medication: Supplements:

Food/Drink	Reaction	Symptoms:
SNACKS	Y / N	
	Y / N	
	Y / N	

Comfort Level 1= normal 10= very uncomfortable ① ② ③ ④ ⑤ ⑥ ⑦ ⑧ ⑨ ⑩

Daily Bowel Movements:
ie: watery, soft, normal, hard etc.

Sleep from: :   to: :   ☐ /hours

Exercise: Cardio Y / N   Weights Y / N

Daily stress Level: (1= calm 10= very stressed)
① ② ③ ④ ⑤ ⑥ ⑦ ⑧ ⑨ ⑩

DAY 6 - WEEK 2 Breakfast/Lunch

Date ___ / ___ / ___

Food/Drink	Time ___:___	Reaction
BREAKFAST		Y / N
		Y / N
		Y / N
		Y / N

Symptoms:

Comfort Level 1= normal 10= very uncomfortable ① ② ③ ④ ⑤ ⑥ ⑦ ⑧ ⑨ ⑩

Notes:

Medication: _____ Supplements: _____

Food/Drink	Time ___:___	Reaction
LUNCH		Y / N
		Y / N
		Y / N
		Y / N

Symptoms:

Comfort Level 1= normal 10= very uncomfortable ① ② ③ ④ ⑤ ⑥ ⑦ ⑧ ⑨ ⑩

Notes:

Medication: _____ Supplements: _____

Food/Drink Time ___ : ___	Reaction	Symptoms:
DINNER	Y / N	
	Y / N	
	Y / N	
	Y / N	

Comfort Level 1= normal 10= very uncomfortable ① ② ③ ④ ⑤ ⑥ ⑦ ⑧ ⑨ ⑩

Notes:

Medication: Supplements:

Food/Drink	Reaction	Symptoms:
SNACKS	Y / N	
	Y / N	
	Y / N	

Comfort Level 1= normal 10= very uncomfortable ① ② ③ ④ ⑤ ⑥ ⑦ ⑧ ⑨ ⑩

Daily Bowel Movements:
ie: watery, soft, normal, hard etc.

Sleep from: :   to: :   ☐ /hours

Exercise: Cardio Y / N   Weights Y / N

Daily stress Level: (1= calm 10= very stressed)
① ② ③ ④ ⑤ ⑥ ⑦ ⑧ ⑨ ⑩

Food/Drink	Time ___ : ___	Reaction	Symptoms:
BREAKFAST		Y / N	
		Y / N	
		Y / N	
		Y / N	

Comfort Level 1= normal 10= very uncomfortable → ① ② ③ ④ ⑤ ⑥ ⑦ ⑧ ⑨ ⑩

Notes:

Medication: Supplements:

Food/Drink	Time ___ : ___	Reaction	Symptoms:
LUNCH		Y / N	
		Y / N	
		Y / N	
		Y / N	

Comfort Level 1= normal 10= very uncomfortable → ① ② ③ ④ ⑤ ⑥ ⑦ ⑧ ⑨ ⑩

Notes:

Medication: Supplements:

DINNER

Food/Drink	Time ___ : ___	Reaction
		Y / N
		Y / N
		Y / N
		Y / N

Symptoms:

Comfort Level 1= normal 10= very uncomfortable ➔ (1)(2)(3)(4)(5)(6)(7)(8)(9)(10)

Notes:

Medication: Supplements:

SNACKS

Food/Drink	Reaction
	Y / N
	Y / N
	Y / N

Symptoms:

Comfort Level 1= normal 10= very uncomfortable ➔ (1)(2)(3)(4)(5)(6)(7)(8)(9)(10)

Daily Bowel Movements:
ie: watery, soft, normal, hard etc.

Sleep from: ___ : ___ **to:** ___ : ___ ☐ /hours

Exercise: Cardio Y / N   Weights Y / N

Daily stress Level: (1= calm 10= very stressed)
(1)(2)(3)(4)(5)(6)(7)(8)(9)(10)

Flick through last week's reports and list out any food, drink or activities that are affecting your condition. The items you list here will provide a summary of triggers you experienced during the week.

Food/Drink

_____

_____

_____

_____

_____

_____

_____

_____

Activity

_____

_____

_____

_____

_____

_____

_____

_____

Tomorrow is a new day!

How has your week been?
Will you be making any changes for next week?

_____
_____
_____
_____
_____
_____
_____
_____
_____
_____
_____
_____
_____
_____
_____
_____

How have you been feeling overall this past week?

WEEK THREE

Date / /

Food/Drink	Time ___:___	Reaction	Symptoms:
BREAKFAST		Y / N	
		Y / N	
		Y / N	
		Y / N	

Comfort Level 1= normal 10= very uncomfortable ① ② ③ ④ ⑤ ⑥ ⑦ ⑧ ⑨ ⑩

Notes:

Medication: Supplements:

Food/Drink	Time ___:___	Reaction	Symptoms:
LUNCH		Y / N	
		Y / N	
		Y / N	
		Y / N	

Comfort Level 1= normal 10= very uncomfortable ① ② ③ ④ ⑤ ⑥ ⑦ ⑧ ⑨ ⑩

Notes:

Medication: Supplements:

Food/Drink	Time ____ : ____	Reaction	Symptoms:
DINNER		Y / N	
		Y / N	
		Y / N	
		Y / N	

Comfort Level 1= normal 10= very uncomfortable ① ② ③ ④ ⑤ ⑥ ⑦ ⑧ ⑨ ⑩

Notes:

Medication: Supplements:

Food/Drink	Reaction	Symptoms:
SNACKS	Y / N	
	Y / N	
	Y / N	

Comfort Level 1= normal 10= very uncomfortable ① ② ③ ④ ⑤ ⑥ ⑦ ⑧ ⑨ ⑩

Daily Bowel Movements:
ie: watery, soft, normal, hard etc.

Sleep from: :   to: :   ☐ /hours

Exercise: Cardio Y / N   Weights Y / N

Daily stress Level: (1= calm 10= very stressed)
① ② ③ ④ ⑤ ⑥ ⑦ ⑧ ⑨ ⑩

DAY 2 - WEEK 3 Breakfast/Lunch

Date ___ / ___ / ___

Food/Drink	Time ___ : ___	Reaction
BREAKFAST		Y / N
		Y / N
		Y / N
		Y / N

Symptoms:

Comfort Level 1= normal 10= very uncomfortable ① ② ③ ④ ⑤ ⑥ ⑦ ⑧ ⑨ ⑩

Notes:

Medication: Supplements:

Food/Drink	Time ___ : ___	Reaction
LUNCH		Y / N
		Y / N
		Y / N
		Y / N

Symptoms:

Comfort Level 1= normal 10= very uncomfortable ① ② ③ ④ ⑤ ⑥ ⑦ ⑧ ⑨ ⑩

Notes:

Medication: Supplements:

DAY 2 - WEEK 3 Dinner/Snacks/Sleep/Wellbeing

Food/Drink   Time _____ : _____   **Reaction**

DINNER

	Reaction
	Y / N
	Y / N
	Y / N
	Y / N

Symptoms:

Comfort Level 1= normal 10= very uncomfortable → ① ② ③ ④ ⑤ ⑥ ⑦ ⑧ ⑨ ⑩

Notes:

Medication: Supplements:

Food/Drink   **Reaction**

SNACKS

	Reaction
	Y / N
	Y / N
	Y / N

Symptoms:

Comfort Level 1= normal 10= very uncomfortable → ① ② ③ ④ ⑤ ⑥ ⑦ ⑧ ⑨ ⑩

Daily Bowel Movements:
ie: watery, soft, normal, hard etc.

Sleep from: ___ : ___ **to:** ___ : ___ ☐ /hours

Exercise: Cardio Y / N   Weights Y / N

Daily stress Level: (1= calm 10= very stressed)
① ② ③ ④ ⑤ ⑥ ⑦ ⑧ ⑨ ⑩

Food/Drink	Time ____ : ____	Reaction
BREAKFAST		Y / N
		Y / N
		Y / N
		Y / N

Symptoms:

Comfort Level 1= normal 10= very uncomfortable ➤ ① ② ③ ④ ⑤ ⑥ ⑦ ⑧ ⑨ ⑩

Notes:

Medication: Supplements:

Food/Drink	Time ____ : ____	Reaction
LUNCH		Y / N
		Y / N
		Y / N
		Y / N

Symptoms:

Comfort Level 1= normal 10= very uncomfortable ➤ ① ② ③ ④ ⑤ ⑥ ⑦ ⑧ ⑨ ⑩

Notes:

Medication: Supplements:

DINNER

Food/Drink Time ____ : ____	Reaction
	Y / N
	Y / N
	Y / N
	Y / N

Symptoms:

Comfort Level 1= normal 10= very uncomfortable ① ② ③ ④ ⑤ ⑥ ⑦ ⑧ ⑨ ⑩

Notes:

Medication: Supplements:

SNACKS

Food/Drink	Reaction
	Y / N
	Y / N
	Y / N

Symptoms:

Comfort Level 1= normal 10= very uncomfortable ① ② ③ ④ ⑤ ⑥ ⑦ ⑧ ⑨ ⑩

Daily Bowel Movements:
ie: watery, soft, normal, hard etc.

Sleep from: :   to: :   ☐ /hours

Exercise: Cardio Y / N   Weights Y / N

Daily stress Level: (1= calm 10= very stressed)
① ② ③ ④ ⑤ ⑥ ⑦ ⑧ ⑨ ⑩

DAY 4 - WEEK 3 Breakfast/Lunch

Date   /   /

BREAKFAST

Food/Drink	Time ___ : ___	Reaction
		Y / N
		Y / N
		Y / N
		Y / N

Symptoms:

Comfort Level 1= normal 10= very uncomfortable ① ② ③ ④ ⑤ ⑥ ⑦ ⑧ ⑨ ⑩

Notes:

Medication: Supplements:

LUNCH

Food/Drink	Time ___ : ___	Reaction
		Y / N
		Y / N
		Y / N
		Y / N

Symptoms:

Comfort Level 1= normal 10= very uncomfortable ① ② ③ ④ ⑤ ⑥ ⑦ ⑧ ⑨ ⑩

Notes:

Medication: Supplements:

Food/Drink   Time _____:_____   Reaction

DINNER

	Reaction
	Y / N
	Y / N
	Y / N
	Y / N

Symptoms:

Comfort Level   1= normal   10= very uncomfortable → ① ② ③ ④ ⑤ ⑥ ⑦ ⑧ ⑨ ⑩

Notes:

Medication: Supplements:

Food/Drink   Reaction

SNACKS

	Reaction
	Y / N
	Y / N
	Y / N

Symptoms:

Comfort Level   1= normal   10= very uncomfortable → ① ② ③ ④ ⑤ ⑥ ⑦ ⑧ ⑨ ⑩

Daily Bowel Movements:
ie: watery, soft, normal, hard etc.

Sleep from: :   to: :   ☐ /hours

Exercise: Cardio Y / N   Weights Y / N

Daily stress Level: (1= calm 10= very stressed)
① ② ③ ④ ⑤ ⑥ ⑦ ⑧ ⑨ ⑩

DAY 5 - WEEK 3 Breakfast/Lunch

Date ___ / ___ / ___

Food/Drink	Time ___ : ___	Reaction
BREAKFAST		Y / N
		Y / N
		Y / N
		Y / N

Symptoms:

Comfort Level 1= normal 10= very uncomfortable ① ② ③ ④ ⑤ ⑥ ⑦ ⑧ ⑨ ⑩

Notes:

Medication: _____ Supplements: _____

Food/Drink	Time ___ : ___	Reaction
LUNCH		Y / N
		Y / N
		Y / N
		Y / N

Symptoms:

Comfort Level 1= normal 10= very uncomfortable ① ② ③ ④ ⑤ ⑥ ⑦ ⑧ ⑨ ⑩

Notes:

Medication: _____ Supplements: _____

Food/Drink   Time _____ : _____   **Reaction**   **Symptoms:**

DINNER

	Reaction
	Y / N
	Y / N
	Y / N
	Y / N

Comfort Level 1= normal 10= very uncomfortable ➞ ① ② ③ ④ ⑤ ⑥ ⑦ ⑧ ⑨ ⑩

Notes:

Medication: Supplements:

Food/Drink   **Reaction**   **Symptoms:**

SNACKS

	Reaction
	Y / N
	Y / N
	Y / N

Comfort Level 1= normal 10= very uncomfortable ➞ ① ② ③ ④ ⑤ ⑥ ⑦ ⑧ ⑨ ⑩

Daily Bowel Movements:
ie: watery, soft, normal, hard etc.

Sleep from: : **to:** : ☐ /hours

Exercise: Cardio Y / N   Weights Y / N

Daily stress Level: (1= calm 10= very stressed)
① ② ③ ④ ⑤ ⑥ ⑦ ⑧ ⑨ ⑩

DAY 6 - WEEK 3 Breakfast/Lunch   Date   /   /

BREAKFAST

Food/Drink Time ____ : ____	Reaction	Symptoms:
	Y / N	
	Y / N	
	Y / N	
	Y / N	

Comfort Level 1= normal
10= very uncomfortable ① ② ③ ④ ⑤ ⑥ ⑦ ⑧ ⑨ ⑩

Notes:

Medication: Supplements:

LUNCH

Food/Drink Time ____ : ____	Reaction	Symptoms:
	Y / N	
	Y / N	
	Y / N	
	Y / N	

Comfort Level 1= normal
10= very uncomfortable ① ② ③ ④ ⑤ ⑥ ⑦ ⑧ ⑨ ⑩

Notes:

Medication: Supplements:

Food/Drink	Time ___ : ___	Reaction	Symptoms:
DINNER		Y / N	
		Y / N	
		Y / N	
		Y / N	

Comfort Level 1= normal 10= very uncomfortable ① ② ③ ④ ⑤ ⑥ ⑦ ⑧ ⑨ ⑩

Notes:

Medication: Supplements:

Food/Drink	Reaction	Symptoms:
SNACKS	Y / N	
	Y / N	
	Y / N	

Comfort Level 1= normal 10= very uncomfortable ① ② ③ ④ ⑤ ⑥ ⑦ ⑧ ⑨ ⑩

Daily Bowel Movements:
ie: watery, soft, normal, hard etc.

Sleep from: :   to: :   ☐ /hours

Exercise: Cardio Y / N   Weights Y / N

Daily stress Level: (1= calm 10= very stressed)
① ② ③ ④ ⑤ ⑥ ⑦ ⑧ ⑨ ⑩

Food/Drink	Time ___:___	Reaction	Symptoms:
BREAKFAST		Y / N	
		Y / N	
		Y / N	
		Y / N	

Comfort Level 1= normal 10= very uncomfortable ① ② ③ ④ ⑤ ⑥ ⑦ ⑧ ⑨ ⑩

Notes:

Medication: Supplements:

Food/Drink	Time ___:___	Reaction	Symptoms:
LUNCH		Y / N	
		Y / N	
		Y / N	
		Y / N	

Comfort Level 1= normal 10= very uncomfortable ① ② ③ ④ ⑤ ⑥ ⑦ ⑧ ⑨ ⑩

Notes:

Medication: Supplements:

Food/Drink	Time ___ : ___	Reaction	Symptoms:
DINNER		Y / N	
		Y / N	
		Y / N	
		Y / N	

Comfort Level 1= normal 10= very uncomfortable ① ② ③ ④ ⑤ ⑥ ⑦ ⑧ ⑨ ⑩

Notes:

Medication: Supplements:

Food/Drink		Reaction	Symptoms:
SNACKS		Y / N	
		Y / N	
		Y / N	

Comfort Level 1= normal 10= very uncomfortable ① ② ③ ④ ⑤ ⑥ ⑦ ⑧ ⑨ ⑩

Daily Bowel Movements:
ie: watery, soft, normal, hard etc.

Sleep from: :   to: :   ☐ /hours

Exercise: Cardio Y / N   Weights Y / N

Daily stress Level: (1= calm 10= very stressed)
① ② ③ ④ ⑤ ⑥ ⑦ ⑧ ⑨ ⑩

Flick through last week's reports and list out any food, drink or activities that are affecting your condition. The items you list here will provide a summary of triggers you experienced during the week.

Food/Drink

_____

_____

_____

_____

_____

_____

_____

_____

_____

Activity

_____

_____

_____

_____

_____

_____

_____

Tomorrow is a new day!

WEEK 3   SUMMARY

How has your week been?
Will you be making any changes for next week?

_____

_____

_____

_____

_____

_____

_____

_____

_____

_____

_____

_____

_____

_____

_____

_____

_____

_____

      How have you been feeling overall this past week?

WEEK FOUR

DAY 1 - WEEK 4 Breakfast/Lunch

Date / /

Food/Drink	Time ___ : ___	Reaction
BREAKFAST		Y / N
		Y / N
		Y / N
		Y / N

Symptoms:

Comfort Level 1= normal 10= very uncomfortable ① ② ③ ④ ⑤ ⑥ ⑦ ⑧ ⑨ ⑩

Notes:

Medication: Supplements:

Food/Drink	Time ___ : ___	Reaction
LUNCH		Y / N
		Y / N
		Y / N
		Y / N

Symptoms:

Comfort Level 1= normal 10= very uncomfortable ① ② ③ ④ ⑤ ⑥ ⑦ ⑧ ⑨ ⑩

Notes:

Medication: Supplements:

DAY 1 - WEEK 4　Dinner/Snacks/Sleep/Wellbeing

Food/Drink	Time ___ : ___	Reaction
DINNER		Y / N
		Y / N
		Y / N
		Y / N

Symptoms:

Comfort Level　1= normal　10= very uncomfortable　① ② ③ ④ ⑤ ⑥ ⑦ ⑧ ⑨ ⑩

Notes:

Medication:　　　　　　　　　Supplements:

Food/Drink	Reaction
SNACKS	Y / N
	Y / N
	Y / N

Symptoms:

Comfort Level　1= normal　10= very uncomfortable　① ② ③ ④ ⑤ ⑥ ⑦ ⑧ ⑨ ⑩

Daily Bowel Movements:
ie: watery, soft, normal, hard etc.

Sleep from:　　:　　to:　　:　　☐ /hours

Exercise:　Cardio Y / N　　Weights Y / N

Daily stress Level:　(1= calm　10= very stressed)
① ② ③ ④ ⑤ ⑥ ⑦ ⑧ ⑨ ⑩

DAY 2 - WEEK 4 Breakfast/Lunch

Date ___ / ___ / ___

Food/Drink	Time ___ : ___	Reaction
BREAKFAST		Y / N
		Y / N
		Y / N
		Y / N

Symptoms:

Comfort Level 1= normal 10= very uncomfortable ① ② ③ ④ ⑤ ⑥ ⑦ ⑧ ⑨ ⑩

Notes:

Medication: _____   Supplements: _____

Food/Drink	Time ___ : ___	Reaction
LUNCH		Y / N
		Y / N
		Y / N
		Y / N

Symptoms:

Comfort Level 1= normal 10= very uncomfortable ① ② ③ ④ ⑤ ⑥ ⑦ ⑧ ⑨ ⑩

Notes:

Medication: _____   Supplements: _____

Food/Drink	Time ___ : ___	Reaction	Symptoms:
DINNER		Y / N	
		Y / N	
		Y / N	
		Y / N	

Comfort Level 1= normal 10= very uncomfortable ① ② ③ ④ ⑤ ⑥ ⑦ ⑧ ⑨ ⑩

Notes:

Medication: Supplements:

Food/Drink	Reaction	Symptoms:
SNACKS	Y / N	
	Y / N	
	Y / N	

Comfort Level 1= normal 10= very uncomfortable ① ② ③ ④ ⑤ ⑥ ⑦ ⑧ ⑨ ⑩

Daily Bowel Movements:
ie: watery, soft, normal, hard etc.

Sleep from: :   to: :   ☐ /hours

Exercise: Cardio Y / N   Weights Y / N

Daily stress Level: (1= calm 10= very stressed)
① ② ③ ④ ⑤ ⑥ ⑦ ⑧ ⑨ ⑩

DAY 3 - WEEK 4 Breakfast/Lunch

Date ___ / ___ / ___

Food/Drink	Time ___:___	Reaction
BREAKFAST		Y / N
		Y / N
		Y / N
		Y / N

Symptoms:

Comfort Level   1= normal   10= very uncomfortable   → ① ② ③ ④ ⑤ ⑥ ⑦ ⑧ ⑨ ⑩

Notes:

Medication: Supplements:

Food/Drink	Time ___:___	Reaction
LUNCH		Y / N
		Y / N
		Y / N
		Y / N

Symptoms:

Comfort Level   1= normal   10= very uncomfortable   → ① ② ③ ④ ⑤ ⑥ ⑦ ⑧ ⑨ ⑩

Notes:

Medication: Supplements:

Food/Drink	Time ___ : ___	Reaction	Symptoms:
DINNER		Y / N	
		Y / N	
		Y / N	
		Y / N	

Comfort Level 1= normal 10= very uncomfortable ① ② ③ ④ ⑤ ⑥ ⑦ ⑧ ⑨ ⑩

Notes:

Medication: Supplements:

Food/Drink	Reaction	Symptoms:
SNACKS	Y / N	
	Y / N	
	Y / N	

Comfort Level 1= normal 10= very uncomfortable ① ② ③ ④ ⑤ ⑥ ⑦ ⑧ ⑨ ⑩

Daily Bowel Movements:
ie: watery, soft, normal, hard etc.

Sleep from: :   to: :   ☐ /hours

Exercise: Cardio Y / N   Weights Y / N

Daily stress Level: (1= calm 10= very stressed)
① ② ③ ④ ⑤ ⑥ ⑦ ⑧ ⑨ ⑩

DAY 4 - WEEK 4 Breakfast/Lunch Date / /

Food/Drink	Time ___ : ___	Reaction
BREAKFAST		Y / N
		Y / N
		Y / N
		Y / N

Symptoms:

Comfort Level 1= normal 10= very uncomfortable → ① ② ③ ④ ⑤ ⑥ ⑦ ⑧ ⑨ ⑩

Notes:

Medication: Supplements:

Food/Drink	Time ___ : ___	Reaction
LUNCH		Y / N
		Y / N
		Y / N
		Y / N

Symptoms:

Comfort Level 1= normal 10= very uncomfortable → ① ② ③ ④ ⑤ ⑥ ⑦ ⑧ ⑨ ⑩

Notes:

Medication: Supplements:

DAY 4 - WEEK 4 — Dinner/Snacks/Sleep/Wellbeing

DINNER

Food/Drink	Time ____ : ____	Reaction
		Y / N
		Y / N
		Y / N
		Y / N

Symptoms:

Comfort Level 1= normal 10= very uncomfortable ① ② ③ ④ ⑤ ⑥ ⑦ ⑧ ⑨ ⑩

Notes:

Medication: Supplements:

SNACKS

Food/Drink	Reaction
	Y / N
	Y / N
	Y / N

Symptoms:

Comfort Level 1= normal 10= very uncomfortable ① ② ③ ④ ⑤ ⑥ ⑦ ⑧ ⑨ ⑩

Daily Bowel Movements:
ie: watery, soft, normal, hard etc.

Sleep from: :   to: :   ☐ /hours

Exercise: Cardio Y / N   Weights Y / N

Daily stress Level: (1= calm 10= very stressed)

① ② ③ ④ ⑤ ⑥ ⑦ ⑧ ⑨ ⑩

Food/Drink	Time ___:___	Reaction	Symptoms:
BREAKFAST		Y / N	
		Y / N	
		Y / N	
		Y / N	

Comfort Level 1= normal 10= very uncomfortable ① ② ③ ④ ⑤ ⑥ ⑦ ⑧ ⑨ ⑩

Notes:

Medication: Supplements:

Food/Drink	Time ___:___	Reaction	Symptoms:
LUNCH		Y / N	
		Y / N	
		Y / N	
		Y / N	

Comfort Level 1= normal 10= very uncomfortable ① ② ③ ④ ⑤ ⑥ ⑦ ⑧ ⑨ ⑩

Notes:

Medication: Supplements:

Food/Drink Time ___ : ___ Reaction

DINNER

Food/Drink	Reaction
	Y / N
	Y / N
	Y / N
	Y / N

Symptoms:

Comfort Level 1= normal 10= very uncomfortable ① ② ③ ④ ⑤ ⑥ ⑦ ⑧ ⑨ ⑩

Notes:

Medication: Supplements:

Food/Drink Reaction

SNACKS

Food/Drink	Reaction
	Y / N
	Y / N
	Y / N

Symptoms:

Comfort Level 1= normal 10= very uncomfortable ① ② ③ ④ ⑤ ⑥ ⑦ ⑧ ⑨ ⑩

Daily Bowel Movements:
ie: watery, soft, normal, hard etc.

Sleep from: :   to: :   ☐ /hours

Exercise: Cardio Y / N   Weights Y / N

Daily stress Level: (1= calm 10= very stressed)
① ② ③ ④ ⑤ ⑥ ⑦ ⑧ ⑨ ⑩

DAY 6 - WEEK 4 Breakfast/Lunch

Date ___ / ___ / ___

Food/Drink	Time ___ : ___	Reaction	Symptoms:
BREAKFAST		Y / N	
		Y / N	
		Y / N	
		Y / N	

Comfort Level 1= normal 10= very uncomfortable ① ② ③ ④ ⑤ ⑥ ⑦ ⑧ ⑨ ⑩

Notes:

Medication: _____ Supplements: _____

Food/Drink	Time ___ : ___	Reaction	Symptoms:
LUNCH		Y / N	
		Y / N	
		Y / N	
		Y / N	

Comfort Level 1= normal 10= very uncomfortable ① ② ③ ④ ⑤ ⑥ ⑦ ⑧ ⑨ ⑩

Notes:

Medication: _____ Supplements: _____

Food/Drink	Time ___ : ___	Reaction	Symptoms:
DINNER		Y / N	
		Y / N	
		Y / N	
		Y / N	

Comfort Level 1= normal 10= very uncomfortable ① ② ③ ④ ⑤ ⑥ ⑦ ⑧ ⑨ ⑩

Notes:

Medication: Supplements:

Food/Drink	Reaction	Symptoms:
SNACKS	Y / N	
	Y / N	
	Y / N	

Comfort Level 1= normal 10= very uncomfortable ① ② ③ ④ ⑤ ⑥ ⑦ ⑧ ⑨ ⑩

Daily Bowel Movements:
ie: watery, soft, normal, hard etc.

Sleep from: :   to: :   ☐ /hours

Exercise: Cardio Y / N   Weights Y / N

Daily stress Level: (1= calm 10= very stressed)
① ② ③ ④ ⑤ ⑥ ⑦ ⑧ ⑨ ⑩

Food/Drink	Time ___ : ___	Reaction	Symptoms:
BREAKFAST		Y / N	
		Y / N	
		Y / N	
		Y / N	

Comfort Level 1= normal 10= very uncomfortable ① ② ③ ④ ⑤ ⑥ ⑦ ⑧ ⑨ ⑩

Notes:

Medication: Supplements:

Food/Drink	Time ___ : ___	Reaction	Symptoms:
LUNCH		Y / N	
		Y / N	
		Y / N	
		Y / N	

Comfort Level 1= normal 10= very uncomfortable ① ② ③ ④ ⑤ ⑥ ⑦ ⑧ ⑨ ⑩

Notes:

Medication: Supplements:

Food/Drink   Time ____ : ____   Reaction

Symptoms:

DINNER		Reaction
		Y / N
		Y / N
		Y / N
		Y / N

Comfort Level 1= normal / 10= very uncomfortable ➤ ① ② ③ ④ ⑤ ⑥ ⑦ ⑧ ⑨ ⑩

Notes:

Medication: Supplements:

Food/Drink   Reaction

Symptoms:

SNACKS		Reaction
		Y / N
		Y / N
		Y / N

Comfort Level 1= normal / 10= very uncomfortable ➤ ① ② ③ ④ ⑤ ⑥ ⑦ ⑧ ⑨ ⑩

Daily Bowel Movements:
ie: watery, soft, normal, hard etc.

Sleep from: :   **to:**   :   ☐ /hours

Exercise: Cardio Y / N   Weights Y / N

Daily stress Level: (1= calm 10= very stressed)
① ② ③ ④ ⑤ ⑥ ⑦ ⑧ ⑨ ⑩

WEEK 4 TRIGGERS

Flick through last week's reports and list out any food, drink or activities that are affecting your condition. The items you list here will provide a summary of triggers you experienced during the week.

Food/Drink

Activity

Tomorrow is a new day!

WEEK 4　SUMMARY

How has your week been?
Will you be making any changes for next week?

_____

_____

_____

_____

_____

_____

_____

_____

_____

_____

_____

_____

_____

_____

_____

_____

_____

How have you been
feeling overall this
past week?

Now you have completed
your weekly reports,
use the following
TRIGGERS ROUND-UP pages
to record all your biggest
triggers from everything
you have found.

Quickly see at a glance all
these triggers and how you
choose to relieve them.

TRIGGERS: ROUND-UP

Review the information you have entered over the last weeks and use the spaces below to enter what you feel are your biggest triggers. Then, if you have methods to relieve yourself, add those in too.

Trigger	Relief Methods

TRIGGERS: ROUND-UP

Trigger	Relief Methods

TRIGGERS: ROUND-UP

Review the information you have entered over the last weeks and use the spaces below to enter what you feel are your biggest triggers. Then, if you have methods to relieve yourself, add those in too.

Trigger	Relief Methods

TRIGGERS: ROUND-UP

Trigger	Relief Methods

TRIGGERS: ROUND-UP

Review the information you have entered over the last weeks and use the spaces below to enter what you feel are your biggest triggers. Then, if you have methods to relieve yourself, add those in too.

Trigger	Relief Methods

TRIGGERS: ROUND-UP

Trigger	Relief Methods

TRIGGERS: ROUND-UP

Review the information you have entered over the last weeks and use the spaces below to enter what you feel are your biggest triggers. Then, if you have methods to relieve yourself, add those in too.

Trigger	Relief Methods

TRIGGERS: ROUND-UP

Trigger	Relief Methods

NOTES

NOTES

NOTES

NOTES

NOTES

NOTES

NOTES

NOTES

NOTES

NOTES

NOTES

NOTES

Made in the USA
Las Vegas, NV
15 March 2022

45701960R00066